BREAKING THE POWER OF INFERIORITY

GREGORY DICKOW

TABLE OF CONTENTS

WHERE IT ALL BEGAN

Introduction

Before Adam and Eve sinned in the Garden of Eden, they were masters over life and over the earth. They were ruled by their spirit and by the Word of God. But after they sinned they were ruled by their feelings. After they sinned they began to be ruled by a sense of inferiority and insecurity—they were powerless! Every negative emotion and reaction that we have is rooted in a sense of powerlessness. When you feel powerless to change a situation in your life or circumstance, you will begin to feel depressed, afraid, angry or discouraged.

All of that comes from a curse passed down from generation to generation . . . a curse of inferiority. In the next few pages we are going to discover true freedom from this curse—freedom from inferiority!

Inferiority is defined as: "a persistent sense of inadequacy. To feel powerless, small, unimportant; to feel as if you fall short."

Romans 3:23 says, *"All have sinned and fallen short of the glory of God."*

- **The word "glory" here means "to become all that God intended you to be".**

- **The term "come short of" means "to be inferior."**

Isn't that interesting? If we put these definitions together properly, the scripture reads: "Because of sin, we have all become inferior to what God originally intended for us to be."

This is the source of just about every weakness and problem in our lives. Man is constantly feeling as if he has come short, or is inferior to God's intention for his life.

With that gnawing feeling of "inferiority," comes a sense of powerlessness. This powerlessness, as mentioned earlier, leads us to feel small. As a result, we try to "build ourselves up" so we don't feel so bad. We jealously compete with others either outwardly or inwardly, and we constantly feel we must look better or be better than someone else, to make those feelings go away. So look at this pattern:

1. "Sin" causes us to fall short of God's intention and approval.

2. Falling short produces a real sense of inferiority.

3. Inferiority sets in and opens wide the floodgates of its offspring (such as insecurity, jealousy, pride, false sense of superiority, racism, etc.).

4. We feel small, so we try to act big; we don't feel as important as someone else, so we exaggerate our sense of importance.

5. We feel powerless, so we get depressed which leads to anger. (Anger is often a manifestation of depression, which comes from a sense of inferiority. When we feel inferior, we use anger as a manipulative force over others to give us a false sense of superiority.)

Now, since "sin" is the cause of inferiority, then until sin is dealt with, there will be no freedom from inferiority or powerlessness and this pattern, in one way or another, will continue in our lives.

The good news is the "sin" problem has been dealt with! *"...Behold the Lamb of God, who takes away the sin of the world" (John 1:29).*

God delivers us from sin by shedding Jesus' blood, thereby dealing with the root cause of inferiority, powerlessness and the curse that has plagued all of our lives. But the blood of Jesus does more than just forgive us from our sin, it restores to us the dominion over life that Adam and Eve once had. Let's take a closer look at that dominion:

Made in God's Image. In Genesis 1:26, God said *"Let Us make man in Our Image, according to Our Likeness, and let them have dominion over the fish of the sea, the foul of the air, the cattle, and OVER ALL THE EARTH..."* God gave man dominion over life, itself.

Listen to David's description of this dominion in Psalm 8:4-6.

"What is man that you are mindful of him, and the son of man that You care for him? Yet you have made him a little lower than God; and You have crowned him with glory and honor. You have made him to have

dominion over the works of Your hands. You have put
all things under his feet!"

Man was supreme. And it is in our genes to desire to be supreme. But when a person is not born again (and often even when they are born again), he unsuccessfully strives for supremacy. He strives for authority. But he is empty inside. He is fragile and inferior due to sin in his heart. He is beat by the devil and by his own fallen nature. So he tries to compensate the inferiority complex by money, by sex, and by power over others! But it is all in vain. There is only one root cause of the inferiority, therefore there is but one root solution. What is it? We will look at it in the coming pages.

THE CURSE OF INFERIORITY

Chapter One

Loss of Dominion. When Adam and Eve sinned, they lost their dominion and their authority. After sinning, they felt rejected, exposed, and naked. They now based their decisions on what they saw and what they felt.

They no longer had dominion over life; it had dominion over them. Listen to this amazing description of the consequence of this spirit of inferiority:

Genesis 3:16. *"To the woman, He said, '...your desire will be for your husband, but he shall rule over you.'"*

Notice, this is a curse. This is not a blessing. What God is actually saying is:

*"Now that you have lost your dominion over life and over the earth, your desire will be to **RULE OVER YOUR HUSBAND**, but he shall **RULE OVER YOU!**"*

It was never God's intention for either of them to rule over each other! It was His intention for both of them to rule over this world, together, as joint heirs, just as we are now joint heirs with Jesus Christ, as described in Romans 8:16.

Dominion vs. Domination. Again, in Genesis 3:16, God says, *"...your desire shall be for your husband, but he shall rule over you."*

With her loss of dominion, she now resorts to domination: *"Your desire for your husband"* is actually translated as, *"you shall desire to dominate your husband, but he will dominate you."*

In exchange for dominion over life, they grasped for domination over each other. How true this still is today! To dominate someone or attempt to manipulate and control someone is a feeble attempt to satisfy our need for dominion. It comes from the inferiority that plagued Adam and Eve after they sinned; then they passed it down to us.

It also says, *"...but he shall rule over you."* Notice, this is a curse too. The curse is: the woman will feel the urge to rule over her husband and, equally, the curse is: the man will feel the need to rule over his wife. (Nowadays, the question is: which one will give in first; but this was not God's intention.) Think about the conflict that many married people experience regarding who is in control. A controlling husband is considered mean and insensitive. A controlling wife is considered having a "Jezebel" spirit. Neither is right. God never intended for either to dominate the other. But we must get to the root if there's to be any change. God never created or designed us to rule over each other. He did create us to rule over all the elements in this earth. He created us to have dominion over things, but he never created us to have dominion over people.

What happens is this inferiority motivates people negatively, as they feel naked and ashamed. Eve felt inferior; she had "fallen" from God's intention and she felt ashamed. Her natural inclination was now to "cover" that inferiority and nakedness by getting control of her husband.

Domination, subjugation, false superiority and racism are all caused by the inner sense of inferiority that we call a "curse".

The Curse of Inferiority. Without the blood of Jesus, we are under this curse of inferiority. The curse of inferiority causes each person to try to control the other, when in fact it's God's will for each person to serve the other. When you are in control of your emotions you will not need to control anyone else.

The same curse that affects marriages affects nations as well. This curse of inferiority was on America when, in its infancy, some among the white race felt like they had to dominate the black race, enslaving them for financial and emotional gain. This domination made some men feel a false sense of superiority. Why did they feel that way? Because on the inside they really felt inferior. There is no justification for the evil of slavery, but the same root cause still exists in America and around the world today. It has cropped up in many cases such as Hitler, trying to dominate the world—out of his false sense of superiority. It tried to crop up through Herod, when he tried to destroy the next generation of children, because he felt the threat of another king coming into power. It cropped up in China when an evil tyrant, Mao Tse-tung—leader of the Gang of Four, who killed somewhere between twenty and sixty-seven million (estimates vary) of his countrymen, including the elderly and intellectuals. Why? Because he was threatened by what he perceived to be their superiority and he could not handle any threats to his power.

Why does it keep cropping up? A crop comes from a seed. And the seed of inferiority is still in the flesh of men. It is in their mind and heart, until they experience the truth that we're sharing.

Why is there still racism in America today? When I ask this question in church services and meetings, there is a quiet hush, because people really don't want to deal with it, but inside, we all know it still lurks. There is racism in America today because people are still under the curse of inferiority and their only concept of being free from inferiority is to feel a sense of superiority over somebody else. False superiority finds fault in others to feed its false ego. But it is truly being fed by inferiority. When one gossips, or criticizes or tears somebody else or another race down, it may muffle the voice of inferiority temporarily, but it does not make it go away. It may make you feel better about yourself for a moment, but it is a lie, and it cannot change you. It's a curse of inferiority.

The real root cause of racism is the spirit of inferiority.

Superiority and Inferiority. Let's talk more specifically about these two emotional forces that do so much damage in our souls. Both of these are actually from the same root—that we discussed earlier: the loss of dominion that came from sin.

Sin disconnects you from God and His approval and wounds the soul. The soul tries to cope in many ways, as we will see later.

Why do people feel inferior? Because the things we were designed by God to have dominion over, actually have dominion over us. War, sickness, and financial instability are some of the forces trying to capitalize on man's inferiority complex, making men afraid.

Often people with the greatest sense of inferiority are the ones who come across as most superior.

The Error of Superiority. The two clearest examples of false superiority that seem to still haunt men's souls, are slavery and Nazi Germany. Hitler had a false sense of the superiority of the Aryan race. Slaveholders had a false sense of superiority in their race, as well. Both of these hideous marks on the history of our world reveal the fallen nature of man.

The Black race was never intended by God to feel inferior or to be inferior to any other race. Similarly, the Germans were never intended by God to feel superior over the rest of the world. There is nothing inferior about being black; but there is nothing superior either. What makes us feel inferior is the devil, sin and our past. But if you are born again, you are a new creature.

Man's Responses To The Curse. As a result of feeling inferior, we usually do one of two things. We either withdraw, become isolated, and live a quiet little life that doesn't make an impact on anybody, or we combat those feelings of inferiority by trying to feel superior.

How do we try to feel superior? First we will try to find something on the outside to make us feel superior—our appearance, talent, or race. Then when that fails, we will try getting a greater education because we think by having a better education at a better university, it will give us some sense of superiority. And when that fails, we think maybe we just need a little more money or a little more popularity, or a little more attention. Then we get a little more money and that doesn't make our inferiority go away. So we think maybe having sex outside of marriage will conquer that sense of inferiority on the inside. *That is where premarital sex comes from—a sense of inferiority.* When a woman who feels inferior thinks she will be loved, she will give herself to a man, sexually. When a man feels like he will make a conquest, he too will sin. Both of these people are reacting to their sense of inferiority.

As you can see, a person goes through all of these things, but none of them work. On the other hand, a person may feel inferior because he hasn't graduated from high school. He may think, "I can't amount to much, since I don't have my degree." It doesn't matter if you don't have your G.E.D. because all you really need is G.O.D.! If God is on your side, there is nothing to feel inferior about. He will cause you to graduate out of defeat and into victory! I am not saying that a great education is bad. I am not saying that you shouldn't pursue it. I am simply saying that it cannot eliminate a sense of inferiority.

The believer may "Christianize" his or her inferiority by saying, "If I get a house like so-and-so; or a new car, then I would be prosperous. After all, God wants me blessed." He does indeed—but not to cover up inferiority.

A preacher may say, "If my church or ministry can grow to a certain size, then I will feel I have succeeded." When that fails, he says, "Well, that person, who has a bigger ministry than me, didn't deserve it" or "he doesn't have to deal with the type of people I have to deal with," or a man may exaggerate the size of his church or his income, to cover up the gnawing feeling of smallness on the inside.

A woman may compare herself to another woman, saying, "Sure, she might look good, but I wonder how much plastic surgery she has had."

A man may say, "I wish I had a wife like her..." referring to someone else's wife. He is comparing his wife to someone else, not because someone else is so much better, but inferiority tells him that he is missing out on something. It tells him that his life is not as good as someone else's.

Another way people deal with inferiority is: boasting, bragging, or projecting an exaggerated appearance of success. If we need to talk about ourselves, there usually isn't much to talk about. That doesn't mean there is never a place for a testimony of what God has done—but we know the difference.

THE SIGNS OF INFERIORITY

Chapter Two

Inferiority takes on many disguises. Some people know that they have it and others don't—but they still have it. They might have a degree of success and find their identity in that. They might have money, or be popular and as a result this gives them confidence. But any confidence that doesn't come from God and His Word, is baseless, and will lead to failure. Jeremiah 17:5 says, *"Cursed is the man who trusts in himself."*

Signs of Inferiority. Allow me to list some signs of inferiority. Certainly, someone (hint, hint!) will come to mind when you look at this list. We can recognize this curse in our lives when we:

1. Grudgingly admit our shortcomings while enthusiastically pointing out those of others.

2. Bully people or talk about others with disdain.

3. Feel attacked when someone disagrees with us.

4. Feel belittled upon receiving correction or confrontation.

5. Blame others for our problems.

6. Derive our worth and value from our performance or appearance.

7. Are touchy, fragile, easily hurt, (whether we show it or not).

8. Are critical and defensive.

9. Feel as if we have to talk about ourselves to get others to like us.

10. Find fault in others so we look better.

If you recognize any of these characteristics in your life, don't panic! We have all been guilty at one time or another. Not only does God forgive you, but we will deal with the root cause and then we will see change!

The Grasshopper Complex. As you probably have read in Numbers 13:31-33, Moses sent twelve spies to scout out the Promised Land. The ten spies came back and said:

"'We are not able to go up against the people; for they are stronger than we...' And they brought up an evil report of the land which they had searched unto the children of Israel, saying, 'The land, through which we have gone to search it, is a land that eateth up the inhabitants thereof; and all the people that we saw in it are men of a great stature. And there we saw the giants, the sons of Anak, which come of the giants: and we were in our own sight as grasshoppers, and so we were in their sight.'"

How these men saw themselves was exactly how others ended up seeing them. They saw themselves small. They saw themselves insignificant. As a result, their hearts melted, their courage was lost and their initiative withered. Many people have lost initiative to do anything significant because they feel small and unimportant.

This is all rooted in inferiority. ***Inferiority is the cause of all failure.*** It causes the fear of failure. An inferior image of ourselves produces bad behavior. As you think within, you will eventually act out on the outside (Proverbs 23:7). The sense of failure and the sense of inferiority come from an image that we have or ourselves—the wrong image. God wants to give us the right image.

In my life, growing up, I had nothing to put stock in. We were the minority in our neighborhood and school. We were Middle-Eastern in a very white, suburban neighborhood. My parents didn't know how to help. They weren't saved and neither was I.

People made fun of my name, my looks, etc. We were different, so we were picked on. I was quiet and to myself. I didn't have any social skills. (I could use some help still, as a matter of fact). But I had no reason to have confidence in my life—until I met Jesus. I was stripped in my soul. I felt naked and stupid and insecure, growing up. There are plenty of things that could have helped me from a natural point of view, but in many ways, I am glad that I didn't receive that help. I didn't have the brains, the looks, or the athletic skill to become popular in school, so I never had any reason to have a false sense of superiority. I faced, day to day, my own inadequacies and insecurities. But by facing them and feeling "naked" in a sense, I didn't have a lot of false securities that I had to let go of, or unlearn. I was ripe for healing. I was ripe for finding real freedom. When Jesus came into my life, I was honest with Him and with myself. I knew He could change me and give me real confidence. I knew with Him on my side, I could overcome anything and be everything He called me to be. I took what the Bible said very literally, right away, because I needed to be "clothed!"

CLOTHED WITH RIGHTEOUSNESS

Chapter Three

A fresh look at righteousness. When Adam and Eve sinned, they were naked, and they knew it. They were inferior right away. They tried to clothe themselves with fig leaves, but it was insufficient. God had to clothe them just so they could make it.

Genesis 3:21. *"The Lord made garments of (animal) skin for Adam and his wife, and clothed them."* You see, no fig leaves that we try to clothe ourselves with will suffice. We need God to clothe us. Notice this verse in Isaiah:

"I will rejoice greatly in the LORD, My soul will exult in my God; For He has clothed me with garments of salvation, He has wrapped me with a robe of righteousness..." (Isaiah 61:10).

Through Jesus Christ, we are clothed with His righteousness. It is His righteousness that raises us up to the position of dominion that Adam and Eve had before they sinned.

2 Corinthians 5:21 says, *"He who knew no sin, was made to be sin for us, that we would be made the righteousness of God."*

In other words, through Jesus death, we become what He was and we become heirs of everything that He deserved. We are now His brethren, not His slaves. Though we didn't deserve it, we have the right to everything that Jesus had—the right to stand in the presence of God without guilt, inferiority or condemnation; and the rights to all of the blessings that were in store for the Firstborn Son.

There is a very powerful story that illustrates this in Genesis 27. You recall when Isaac was old and wanted to bless his sons. Esau was the firstborn and was in line for Isaac's greater blessing. But while Esau was hunting, Jacob plotted with his mother to "steal" the rights of the firstborn and the blessing. His father was old and could not see well. So they put hairy animal skin on his hands so that when his father reached out and touched him, he would think it was Esau. Of course, it worked, and the rest is history. As unfair as it may seem, it is a picture of how unfairly Jesus, the firstborn, was treated for us, so that His skin could cover us, so that when we come to God, through Jesus, God will feel the skin of His Son upon us and bless us with the blessings of the Firstborn!

What a marvelous picture of being clothed with something greater than ourselves, to cover our spiritual nakedness, our emotional nakedness, and take our place next to Jesus—with His authority, His dominion and His "glory"!

Are you catching this now? We are clothed with His righteousness, and as a result, our inferiority, shame and nakedness is done away with! Since sin disconnects us from God, we can react in one of two ways. We can cover ourselves with our own false sense of approval and superiority or we can receive His righteousness!

Mastery Over Life. When we are born again and receive His righteousness, we are reunited with our original authority, because we are reunited with the Author. We are reunited with our original mastery over life because we are reunited with the Master.

Here is a revealing name given to Jesus by His disciples—Master. Master means "one who controls or influences events or things." When He healed the sick, they called Him "Master." When He calmed the storm, they called Him "Master." When He forgave the unforgivable, they called him "Master."

Paul, the apostle, said that he strove for the mastery of his body, his thoughts and his life. (1 Corinthians 9:24-26).

Think of some of the statements God makes in the Word, implying **His desire for our superiority over life, not over people.**

- Luke 10:19. *"Behold I give you authority."*

- 2 Corinthians 10:5. *"Taking every thought captive."*

- Genesis 1:28. *"Fill the earth. Rule the earth. Subdue the earth."*

- Deuteronomy 8:1. *"Possess the land."*

- Mark 16:17. *"Cast out devils"*

- Matthew 18:18. "*Whatsoever you bind on earth, shall be bound in heaven; whatsoever you loose on earth, shall be loosed in heaven.*"

- Psalm 115:16. "*The heavens are the Lord's, but the earth He has given to the sons of men.*" *(That's you and me!)*

The list goes on and on, because God has designed us to be in control, but not to be controlling. When someone has a "controlling" personality, it is rooted in this inferiority. When we feel inferior, we attempt to control others. Competitive jealousy is often the outcome (which we will deal with in a later chapter).

The Solution to Inferiority. Just as we discussed how the loss of dominion leads to our attempts to dominate others, it also leads to a glaring sense of inferiority. Though many are good at masking this complex, its insidious poison is in every fallen man. Again, that's why Jesus said, "You must be born again." And though you may be born again, the soul needs to be renewed, transformed by the washing that comes from the Word of God.

But the key here is in understanding that His righteousness is the greatest gift we can possibly receive when we are born again. Romans 5:17 says *"Through the abundance of grace and the gift of righteousness, we reign in life."* The Amplified translation says that through righteousness *"we reign as kings in this life."*

So we see here that righteousness causes us to **REIGN**. This is what restores our superiority in this life. But remember, this is not superiority over people. It is superiority over life and its circumstances. It is superiority over sin, sickness, fear, anxiety, depression, discouragement and every other negative emotion and circumstance that we ever face.

ROYALTY DESTROYS INFERIORITY

Chapter Four

These three powerful words should be etched in your mind forever:

Royalty destroys inferiority!

What does that mean? Very simply, a king is inferior to no one! Of course, Jesus is the King of Kings. He lived His life with no complex, with no inferiority, with no insecurity. That's why He was able to say to His disciples, *"the Son of man did not come to be served, but to serve!"* (Matthew 20:28). Jesus was able to serve others because He was not insecure. He knew who He was and that released Him into being a blessing to those He came in contact with. Insecurity makes us selfish—we are so concerned about ourselves (how we look, what we have, how we compare to others, etc.), that we are in bondage. We see others as a threat, rather than as our brother or sister or friend.

Revelation 1:6 declares that Jesus *"has made **us** kings and priests unto God and His Father."* This is an amazing scripture. We are made "kings" by Jesus Christ! We are in the ***ROYAL FAMILY! WE ARE PART OF THE ROYAL BLOOD LINE.*** A king or a queen has a revelation that they are in dominion. They are not inferior!

As a believer, you have been placed in the Royal Family. You are of Royal Blood. You are a King in God.

So many people have their identity wrapped up in their position in this life, their economic or social status, their fame or fortune . . . yet none of those represent true royalty. When the body of Christ truly gets a hold of our royalty in Christ Jesus, we will not only walk free from the effects of inferiority, we will finally walk in the power that Jesus promised we would walk in. If we are royalty, then we are no longer inferior. Royalty destroys inferiority, because it changes who we are.

Yes, but does it deal with the sin problem?

I'm glad you asked! Remember earlier, we looked at 2 Corinthians 5:21, *"He who knew no sin, was made to be sin for us, that we would be made the righteousness of God in Him."*

So "righteousness" deals with the sin problem; and we are now clothed in righteousness through the blood of Jesus.

Well, righteousness doesn't just put any old clothing on us, it puts **ROYAL** clothing on us. Watch more closely what God says in Romans 5:17...

*"For if because of one man's trespass, death reigned through that one, much more surely will those who receive God's overflowing grace and the free gift of righteousness **REIGN AS KINGS IN LIFE** through the one Man Jesus Christ."*

Righteousness makes us kings! **Therefore, righteousness delivers us from inferiority.** A person who has the signs of inferiority is a person who has not really understood this amazing gift of righteousness. Allow me to shed a little more light on its meaning.

What is righteousness? Righteousness is the ability to stand in the presence of God without a sense of guilt, inferiority, or condemnation. It's to stand in His presence as if sin had never been. That's how Adam and Eve stood with God before they sinned. Before they became "emotionally ruled" people, they reigned in life. They reigned as kings in life. There was no inferiority complex. There was no sense of guilt or condemnation. There was no discouragement or depression. They were on top of the world.

The beautiful thing is, that it was all restored to us when Jesus, who knew no sin, was made to be sin for us that we would be made the righteousness of God in Him.

If you are born again, you are now the righteousness of God. You are the head and not the tail, above only and not underneath!

Jesus' authority is your authority! Jesus spoke to the elements of this world and they obeyed Him. He commanded the wind to stop and it did. He commanded the fig tree to bear no fruit and it withered up. He told his disciples where to put down the net and 153 fish immediately hearkened to His command!

Well, this wasn't the first time that a man mastered the elements. In 1 Kings 17:1, Elijah commanded the rain to stop and it didn't rain for three and a half years until he permitted it.

James 5:17 tells us that Elijah had a nature like ours. In other words, we can do what he did. That's great, but Jesus went one step further. He said in John 14:12 *"the works that I do, shall you do also; and greater works!"*

What an amazing statement for Jesus to make. We will do greater works than He did! But if we cannot get control of what's on the inside of us, it will be very difficult to get control of what's on the outside.

Too often, we are frustrated by the things on the outside of us that are out of control. We do everything in our power to change those things, at times to no avail. Even if we are able to manipulate things and change them to our satisfaction, we still are not happy.

Why? Because it's not what's happening on the outside that determines our peace and happiness—it's what's happening on the inside.

We see Jesus mastering life around Him, but we fail to realize that it was a direct result of his mastery on the inside—his freedom from inferiority. Jesus was in total control of His attitudes, His words, and His thought life.

I don't want you to be discouraged right now, by thinking that you could never attain to that. That's not the point here. You have to see the correlation. *As He is, so are you in this world* (1 John 4:17). Since Jesus was a King in this life, He mastered life. It was His righteousness that gave Him His royalty; and you are carrying the same righteousness, therefore the same royalty, in you. It gives you the same power that He had. You are no longer powerless, therefore, you can do what He did. But remember, His power came from a real sense of dominion. It came from within. He had no inferiority complex because He knew who He was. When you accept these things about yourself, you will begin walking in the same power—from within. Righteousness, royalty and dominion will create a power in you, a control in you, that will deliver you from feeling insecure and trying to control others around you. You now possess self-control, which is one of the most powerful forces in the universe.

Remember, Proverbs 16:32 says, *"Better is a man who can rule his own spirit than one who can capture a city."* Well, Jesus didn't just capture a city—He captured a world! He was able to because of His capacity to rule Himself, from within, enabling Him to be completely free from inferiority.

Jesus was human, like you and I. He was tempted in all things as we are, yet without sin. He had the same opportunity to get mad at His brothers as you do; to retaliate when mistreated, like you do. His disciples even wanted to call down fire and consume those that did not follow Him. But Jesus refrained. He had a cool spirit.

He understood who He was. Proverbs 17:27 says, *"He who has a cool spirit is a man of understanding."* In other words, you can only be cool when you have an understanding of who you are. Jesus did; and now, clothed with His righteousness, so can you!

A Portion Reserved for You

Chapter Five

Freedom From Comparisons. As I stated earlier, we must deal with the insecurity that accompanies inferiority. Now that you understand your righteousness, your royalty, your dominion, you should be sensing the shackles of inferiority breaking off of you!

But often times, we compare ourselves with others, because we still have the tendency to feel a bit insecure about what we have or what we have done. Jealousy and envy are the offspring of insecurity—and we have all felt jealous at one time or another. Be aware, however, that jealousy is to our power, what kryptonite was to Superman's power!

There are 5 side effects to jealousy that God does not want you to experience ever again.

1. **Jealousy makes you powerless.**

   1 Corinthians 3:3 says *"...for as long as there are envying and jealousy among you, are you not unspiritual, walking as MERE men?"* (We are not "mere" men, we are "kings." But when we walk in jealousy, it lowers our class and we no longer walk as kings.)

2. **Jealousy makes you cruel.** Song of Solomon 8:6 says, *"Jealousy is as cruel as the grave".*

3. **Jealousy brings confusion.** (James 3:16).

4. **Jealousy makes you bitter.** (James 3:14).

5. **Jealousy cuts off your future.** (Proverbs 23:17-18).

As you can see, these are very telling fruits of jealousy, which are rooted in insecurity.

When the children of Israel asked God for a king, He gave them Saul. (Of course, God wanted to be their King, and he wanted to make them kings, as He has made us, in Christ Jesus.) 1 Samuel 9:1-2 tells us that Saul was head and shoulders above anyone else. He was a powerful and handsome man. It says that there was not a more handsome man in all of Israel. He would certainly have been at the top of People's 50 most beautiful people!

But his "superior" attributes did not make him immune to inferiority and insecurity. God knew this and He wanted Saul to succeed. As a result, God strategically orchestrated a meal for Saul with the prophet Samuel, so that Saul could be prepared for the insecurity he would certainly face as king. Let's look at what happened.

1 Samuel 9:22-24 says:

*"And Samuel took Saul and his servant, and brought them into the parlour, and made them sit in the chiefest place among them that were invited, which were about 30 persons. And Samuel said to the cook, "Bring the portion which I gave you, of which I said, 'Set it aside!' And the cook lifted **the honored portion**, and set it before Saul, saying, 'See what was reserved for you. Eat, for until the hour appointed it was kept for you, ever since I invited all the people.' So Saul ate that day with Samuel."*

You may say, "what in the world does that have to do with insecurity, and how can that apply to me?"

It's very simple: After becoming king, Saul was faced with the threatening feelings that David would usurp him as king and try to take everything Saul had. Later, they sang of Saul and they sang of David, saying "Saul has conquered thousands and David has conquered tens of thousands." This curled Saul's blood with jealousy and from that point on, he tried to kill David, sacrificing his own royalty and blessing in exchange for his jealousy. I wonder how much of our royalty we have sacrificed in exchange for our feelings of jealousy, when we feel threatened by someone else's success.

This is when Saul should have remembered the experience he had with God and with Samuel, when God was saying to him, "I have set aside a portion for you! I have reserved it for you and I have kept it for you. No matter what anyone else has, no matter what happens, no matter who comes along after you, *I have reserved a portion for you!* You never have to feel threatened by anyone else's success, because I have reserved a portion for you. You never have to be jealous of anyone else, because I have reserved a por-tion for you. No matter what it looks like, no matter how many people look like they have more, or they seem more successful, know for certain, Saul, that I have reserved a portion for you. No matter what you think right now, I have reserved a portion for you."

God wanted that etched in Saul's mind forever! Saul forgot that experience—that revelation. Make sure you don't. God is saying the same thing to you. This will free you from jealousy, insecurity, and inferiority.

There is a portion for you. And it is an honored portion. It is a kingly portion. That doesn't mean that others won't be blessed. There is enough success, blessing, and royalty to go around for everyone. But you must know God has thought this thing through. No matter what it looks like, no matter what you feel, you are royalty. There is an honored portion for you, as you meditate on your royalty—on your righteousness. As soon as you do, you will drop all comparisons, all jealousy and you will never again have to bring someone down to feel good about yourself. You will never again have to walk in inferiority again. You will never have to feel the shame of being different or feeling less than anyone else. You are a king! You are Royalty.

Think it. Speak it. Act it. Walk in it! And you will never be the same again!

ABOUT THE AUTHOR

Gregory Dickow is the host of "Changing Your Life," a dynamic television show seen throughout the world, reaching a potential half a billion households. He is also the founder and Senior Pastor of Life Changers International Church, a diverse and thriving congregation in the Chicago area with several thousand in weekly attendance.

Known for his ability to communicate the power and principles of God's Word clearly and concisely, Pastor Dickow lives to see the lives of people dramatically changed forever.

Pastor Dickow is also the host of "Ask the Pastor" a live radio show reaching the world through radio and the internet with live callers asking hard-hitting questions about their real-life problems. Pastor Dickow is reaching people personally, encouraging them and empowering them to succeed in every area of life.

Other Books Available by Pastor Gregory Dickow

- Acquiring Beauty
- Breaking the Power of Inferiority
- Conquering Your Flesh
- Financial Freedom
- How to Hear the Voice of God
- How to Never Be Hurt Again
- Taking Charge of Your Emotions
- The Power to Change Anything
- Winning the Battle of the Mind

Audio Series available by Pastor Gregory Dickow

- Financial Freedom: Strategies for a Blessed Life
- How to Pray & Get Results
- Love Thyself
- Mastering Your Emotions
- Redeemed from the Curse
- The Blood Covenant
- Building Your Marriage God's Way

You can order these and many other life-changing materials by calling toll-free 1-888-438-5433.

For more information about Gregory Dickow Ministries and a free product catalog, please visit *www.changinglives.org*